C

ESSENTIAL POETS SERIES 158

Canada Council for the Arts   Conseil des Arts du Canada

Guernica Editions Inc. acknowledges the support of
the Canada Council for the Arts.

BRIAN DAY

CONJURING JESUS

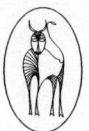

GUERNICA
TORONTO — BUFFALO — CHICAGO — LANCASTER (U.K.)
2009

Copyright © 2009, by Brian Day and Guernica Editions Inc.
All rights reserved. The use of any part of this publication, reproduced, transmitted in any form
or by any means, electronic, mechanical, photocopying, recording or otherwise stored in a
retrieval system, without the prior consent of the publisher is an infringement of the copyright
law.

Antonio D'Alfonso, editor
Guernica Editions Inc.
P.O. Box 117, Station P, Toronto (ON), Canada M5S 2S6
2250 Military Road, Tonawanda, N.Y. 14150-6000 U.S.A.

Distributors:
University of Toronto Press Distribution,
5201 Dufferin Street, Toronto (ON), Canada M3H 5T8

Gazelle Book Services, White Cross Mills, High Town,
Lancaster LA1 4XS U.K.

Independent Publishers Group,
814 N. Franklin Street, Chicago, Il. 60610 U.S.A.

First edition.
Printed in Canada.

Legal Deposit – Fourth Quarter
Library of Congress Catalog Card Number: 2008928102
Library and Archives Canada Cataloguing in Publication
Day, Brian
Conjuring Jesus / Brian Day.
(Essential poets series ; 158)
Poems.
ISBN 978-1-55071-274-2
1. Jesus Christ — Poetry. I. Title. II. Series.
PS8557.A916C57 2008   C811'.6   C2008-902882-1

Contents

Jesus, Son of David 7
The Conversion of Jesus 9
Jesus and the Foreign 11
Spit and Blindness 12
Jairus' Daughter 13
Healed of Haemorrhages 15
Jesus Seeking Solitude 16
Jesus, Suicidal 18
Jesus Considers Amputation 20
Corruption 21
Weeds 22
Open Party 23
Tax Collectors 24
Snake of God 25
The Mother of Jesus 27
Enemies 28
The Forgiving Manager 30
Talents 31
The Planter 33
Flower and Flight 34
Indolence 36
Children and the Kingdom 38
Reversals 39
Good News 40
Again 41
Perfume 42
Better Not to Marry 44

A Woman Caught in Adultery 46
Jesus, Versatile 48
Jesus, Praying 50
The Transfiguration 52
Lazarus 55
Jesus Enters Jerusalem 56
Bread of His Body 57
The Beloved Disciple 58
Judas 59
Pilate's Wife Dreams of Jesus 61
Pilate 62
A Soldier Questions Jesus 63
The Beloved and Mary at the Cross 64
Jesus, Forsaken 65
Corpse 66
The Angel at the Tomb 67
After 68
Peter, Swimming 69
Thomas 71
As I Have Loved You 73
Appearances 75
Jesus Not Contained in His Book 76

Biblical References 79
Acknowledgements 81

Jesus, Son of David

The gospels begin with the naked
proclamation that Jesus is first the son
of David. And Jesus could hardly claim
for a model – or for the opening line
of his story – a man
with a more scandalous, unseemly past.

David is pacing on the roof of his palace
when he spies, like the liquids of all his dreams,
a woman shimmering with the rituals of her bath.
He watches her pouring of oils to water,
her sleek limbs rising from those tiny
warm waves; sends servants to summon
this beauty to his chamber. He plunges
to the fabulous sin of adultery,
the act that stands in his religion
as the carnal emblem of defection from God.

Years before his stint as a royal voyeur,
David's desires are stirred by the kingdom's sweet
beguiling prince. He wears Jonathan's clothing as a charm
on his skin, and wraps himself in the prince's scent.
He kisses him in secret when they meet in a field
and offers him the forbidden wild honey
of his heart. When his adored is slaughtered in war,
David, crooning in eulogy, divulges
that the touch and taste and scent

of this man exceed the most
he has known with concubines or wives.

David makes worship a burlesque performance,
dancing in the raw to honour his God
and scattering freely to watching women
the sight of his regal bouncing genitalia –
abandoning every semblance of discretion
in his wild religious physical joy.

David is, perhaps worst of all, a poet:
forging exaltation from image and syllable,
twisting religion into the rhythms of verse,
and remaking the shifting weather of his moods
to the arcing psalms of a nation's scripture.

This is Jesus' genetic allotment. The lines
of his story are infected
with the deviant legacy of David. Half
a verse in, and we have been warned.

The Conversion of Jesus

Jesus arrives onstage at age thirty, the gospels
swallowing like a camel all the secrets
of his past. He's at a river, for forgiveness,
standing in line with the dregs of his nation.
There's a story to that, and Jesus,
once it's smoothed in his hands, will tell it.

Like the son who'll be called the prodigal, Jesus
had squandered every cent of his religious
inheritance on the ritual equivalent
of harlots and wine: cruising among polished
pagan idols, contorting his mouth
to foreign devotions, and savouring
apostasy's myriad flavours. He'd embarked
on a descent through cantos
of depravity, moulting each restriction of his
bleak old religion – sunken till
no rung was left beneath him and he
was kept by the keeper of pigs.

His mind bristled with forbidden images of God,
and each figure he had added to himself in exile
now limned the contours of what he had lost.
One day he awakes in the grip
of a hunger and needs to inhabit the long-
discarded stories of his youth, that familiar
tradition enscripted in his blood. What

he seeks in naive religious greed
is more: not to make a further trade of property
but to have both hands of his tugging soul
stuffed with all the coins they can hold.

This is not permitted in the rule books of repentance –
and he composes some token prayer
of contrition, rehearsing its stilted
deliberate phrases as he walks the tortuous
road toward his home. Then,
like a page as it lifts from a dream,
the life he's abandoned runs shamelessly
toward him, its arms outstretched, his name
in welcome resounding from its tongue. And this lost world
kisses him: like a father, like a dove. He is stunned
to become a beloved son, and the favour
of the heavens clothes him in light,
in the cherished robe and ring of family.
His practised confession is swept aside,
a feast is ordered, musicians called,
and he, to his bafflement, is more adored
than if he had stayed and done labour
at home. He embraces the reprobate friends
of his youth, tucks in to the browned
and golden calf, feasting and flirting and
buoyant with wine, immersed in every
sensual pleasure that had lured him
to stray from his father's house.

There is not a whisper of his regret.

Jesus and the Foreign

It begins with the blessed assault of robbers
   who plunder his body with a fistful of knives,
club and kick and bash in his skin
   till he crumples at their feet like a spoiling of fruit,
his flesh tattooed to the dark hues of figs.
   What restores him is not his own family or village –
not the passing priests of his own religion –
   but the stranger who is moved by the sight of his body
and stops to soothe his ragged wounds
   with the generous pouring of oil and wine.
This stranger like an angel washes Jesus' body
   and presses him with healing Jesus has not known.
He wraps him like a treasure in the ribbons of his shirt,
   scoops him tenderly like a great sleeping child,
drapes his limp body on the donkey's back,
   and murmurs the lullaby of man to suffering man.

Jesus wakes in a place that is neither his home
   nor a foreign city, but the border of the holy
with the vast profane. In the inn between them,
   he drifts on the verges of waking and dream,
redeemed by the foreign and with eyes in both worlds.
   He has surrendered to intimate, outlandish ministrations,
a stranger's hands have eased him past the limits of belief,
   and the inestimable cost of his recovery is paid.

Spit and Blindness

When a blind man is brought to Jesus to be healed,
  Jesus closes his eyes and recalls his own blindness;
then leads him to a tree just beyond the town,
  feeling the man's trust on his arm as they walk.
Jesus smears viscous spit on the lids of his eyes,
  smoothing it like kohl to the other man's skin,
for there is nothing too vile to make a man whole.
  Jesus, sensing beauty, does not open his eyes
but touches as a blind man reads another man's face,
  and each of them, blind, leads the other one forward.
Jesus needs the guidance of the blind man's vision,
  needs to see the world from the other man's skull –
for if the blind do not lead, how will anyone see?
  The other man tells him that men are like trees,
erect and fluttering, blurred at their edges –
  an aura of light like leaves on their skin.
Jesus holds to the side of the patient man's face
  and they pitch as two men in the tent of their twilight.
Again Jesus spreads wetness on the eyes of the man
  and again, his eyes closed, imagines sight.
The world of the once-blind man clicks into focus:
  Jesus' face before him cut clear as a leaf.

Jairus' Daughter

He had murmured words like the chant
    in a game, words I might have mistaken
        for my name. It was like waking
from sleep – or to it, this man
    standing angelic by the side
        of my bed, as if I'd been born
with a second father, the colours
    of the room still glowing and soft,
        the edges of his body like the wing-tips
of birds. I saw flautists and mourners
    lined up at my door, lips poised
        with the quilting melodies of death,
their instruments warming as my body
    cooled, and filling with breath as breath
        left my lungs. The pain, I discovered,
had abandoned my body, lifted
    like fine morning mist from my skin.
        My legs longed to dash over paths
and fields, gaming and dancing like a bird
    hugged by sun. He asked me to rise,
        his arms like my mother's
drew me up gently to where
    I fit smoothly in the cloth
        of myself. He requested my meal,
sat at my bedside and stroked
    my hair. Colours were as milky
        as the light in his eyes,

and I was his beautiful
 daughter, marrying this moment
  I had not before known.

Healed of Haemorrhages

I had chased the shadows of healers through Palestine,
    and though each took my payment, none offered relief.
My body bloomed, yielding nothing but pain,
    that swelling that consumed me with an excess of myself.
This Jesus had a legend of scriptural proportions,
    his cures now hale and proclaiming wherever I travelled.
Rumour had it he stank of fishermen and God,
    that his touch washed out the stains that had clung to
        one's life.
I traced his itinerary till I was part of the press
    of the hobbling and infirm, all pleading for his mercy.
The flash of his profile as he pushed through the crowd –
    I reached, and touched like a soothing fire
the fabric of his cloak. I was, simply, healed,
    my blood flowing decently back through my veins.
I knew a new life was conceived within me
    and knew that new life was solely mine.
He sensed that someone had tapped his reservoir of virtue,
    nabbed me like a child caught filching a sweet.
Faith, he said, was what had healed me.
    Yes, of course – but not faith in him:
more faith that any man or cloak might heal;
    a faith as indiscriminate and catholic as the air.
I did not sign up as one of his followers
    as they hoarded and debated his cryptic words.
His sayings were not well-fitted to my ears.
    Healthy, I had no more need of doctors.

Jesus Seeking Solitude

He'd relied too much on the common coin
of magic, saw that most of those who followed him
recalled nothing else. There were hordes
who touched him only to steal, to sponge
his dwindling presence and power, to witness
and report on his circus acts of healing.
He hated each one of their meagre minds.
Addicted to miracles, they would follow
him anywhere to see one more –
but discarded his every crafted word,
words as useless to them as chaff.

He craved the blue
of mountaintops and mornings, temples
untouched by human greed,
would rise before light
to drink in their stillness.
At times he'd touch heaven
in the cool of the dawn,
be washed in a flow
of silence and imminent
words. He'd know a trembling
order in the world, a current
and pulse like the cadence of psalms.

But these hours were a quickly corroded treasure.
The feast of his heaven would be overturned,
dogs ripping the delicate dishes in their jaws
and leaving them glistening with slaver and need. Still
intuitions would shatter like glass, and he'd
fall like lightning from heaven to earth,
the pearls of his solitude trampled by swine.

Jesus, Suicidal

He's perched, early morning, on the edge of the temple,
the parapet unsteadying him with impulse and height.
He cannot play the parts he has glimpsed for himself,
or contain all his longings in the skin of one man.
A legion of demons is teeming inside him,

and he pictures that plummet down toward stone
in an arc like the pouring of pigs from a cliff.
His patchwork life is screaming at its seams –
a congeries of opposites that will not cohere –
and he can't hold to each fractious sheep of his will

or shape them to the order of a docile herd.
And he breaks the shepherd's cardinal rule,
leaving the flock in his charge unprotected,
tracking one dissenting, recalcitrant ram,
following its track through unfrequented brush.

He sights it grazing on its own lush plot
and steers it, ambivalent, back to the pasture.
He fears the scattering of the flock in his absence,
but the hands of thieves and the teeth of wolves
have left his unguarded sheep untouched.

Giddy with the undeserved fullness of his flock,
he wants only to celebrate his blazing good fortune,
to summon every shepherd and servant he knows
and host a long night of reeling and wine.
Jesus, the bad shepherd, has been spared devastation.

He has sampled new folly, and risk has enriched him.
Now he stands balanced on the edge of the temple,
a man in possession of each fraction of his flock.
Not a single demon has been stripped from his skin,
and he shepherds them all to the temple's shore.

Jesus Considers Amputation

The eyes, those organs of lust
    and adultery – gouge them out.
The penis, that half-blind homunculus
    that leads men inevitably
    into the ditch – slice it off.
Chop off the hands that itch with greed.
Remove at the ankle the feet
    that lead to alleys that stink of sin.
Carve out the lips and clip off the tongue
    that crave the excesses of flesh
    and food, that sully the body
    with blasphemous words.
Cut off every part of you that sins
    and see what you've got left.
If you have any ears
    left to hear with, then hear.

Corruption

A woman conceals defiling yeast
within barrelfuls of flour, mixing
and stirring in corruption's kitchen.

The yeast festers and foments within
the dough, the spores of the foreign
breeding to some fantastic Babylon

of bread, expanding to loaves
that might feed a multitude and infect
an entire hillside with heresy.

The weed of mustard scars
the garden, its gold erupting rudely
on the skin of the land, blessing

with its blight of wild contagion.
A single whore contaminates a dinner,
salting an assembly till all

are flavoured. The offensive
are cherished, reversing
the word that was given on Sodom:

for a handful of sinners
will the people be saved. It is
our corruption that washes us clean.

Weeds

A rival has sown my fields with weeds,
    and I let them grow there among the grain.
My neighbours deride me, call me an imbecile:
    hard work but they must be pulled out by their roots.
But they, like so many weeds, are admirable,
    resolute in rooting where they were not welcomed
and clinging to a land they mark as their own.
    I am, I admit, fond of them –
as I've grown fond of my favourite old vices
    that some days threaten to choke me to death
and on others delight me with their seasons of bloom.
    I won't force this soil to bear only one fruit
or hoe the tares from the fields of my flesh.
    I am a man enriched by my sins,
and when with my grain I harvest my weeds,
    mine will be the highest bonfire of thanks.

Open Party

A partyer himself, conspicuous from the start
for his eating and drinking, he offers a reveller's
view of redemption. Heaven is a party
without set places, where we're all at the level
of welcome guests. Wine flows liberally,
tables are weighed with exotic dishes,
and the guests – both the wealthy and the rabble
collected from the streets – share in the permissive,
promiscuous measures of the dance.
We are here without account of our merit,
pressing against those we'd not glance
at in the street – and this party's a rarity,
a suspension that holds us glowing in its hands
as it offers us eyes for what we'd not seen:
the pleasures of sliding to our own promised land –
this delicious, indiscriminate version of heaven.

Tax Collectors

Jesus consorts with his nation's traitors,
who squeeze the poor to pay out tax.
Jesus talks back to his traitors' haters –
tells them to get off the tax men's backs.

He frequently visits the tables of sinners,
brushes fingers with women of the lowest repute,
loves the food they serve at sinners' dinners
and does not as he lies on their couches rebuke

them for the wicked lives they enjoy.
The progressives repeatedly try to bait him
but Jesus, an unscrupulous party boy, is coy.
The righteous and leftists have reason to hate him.

Snake of God

The tiny bones of Moses' ears
had echoed with the absolute commandment
of God: forbidden were statues
in animal forms. Then the Israelites
again were complaining against God,
and the Almighty's spite twined the earth with snakes,
infecting the unfaithful with slow-burning venom.

But when God repented of this poisonous anger,
it was Moses who received in his mouth
God's stark contradiction, the instruction
to fashion from fired bronze the curative
curving figure of a snake. This
was the remedy for such a divinely inspired
disease. Moses obliged, holding up the sinuous
shape in the wilderness. And the Israelites,
as they beheld its violation, were healed.

Jesus is held up
                in a more modern time
to heal those whom God's
                            own violence has stricken.
He's as darling as Moses,
                      as immune from prosecution,
a sanctioned revision
                to the Holy One's rules.

Jesus is as brazen
                as God's own idolatry,
his power of healing
                    forged in heresy.
He's incarnate as the twisting
                      snake of God
and slips this smoothly
                        through his listeners' hands.

The Mother of Jesus

He could pull a boatload of fish from his sleeve
and his mother would see only the naive
little boy whose eyes grew wide
with tales of wonder and who kept cutting
his fingers on the edges of the real.
She'd shake her motherly head
in dismay, and chide him for living
in a madman's world.

She is not his mother.
The only ones who deserve
to be called his mother
are those who hang
on each phrase he speaks.
He will not be held captive
by some accident of birth or let
one woman's dullness determine
who he is. It is his friends
who are his mother. They feed him
with the blessed breasts
of their attention, and it is
in their rocking arms he grows strong.

Enemies

Jesus has several. His years
of being abused as a bastard
have left him with the hard scar tissue
of hatred. He detests
those who mock him, hurls their bitterness
back in their faces, spits out
that they are nothing but hypocrites.
He calls them show-offs and pokes
at each speck they carry in their eyes.

His hatred hangs as a millstone
about his neck, and he cannot re-enter his revels
with God. The only recourse he has is language,
and he coins the koan: *Love your enemies.*
It sounds as likely as a caravan
of camels through a needle's eye.
This is the phrase he nurtures daily,
manuring it like a gardener, and tasting failure
more times than he can count.

It is as he fingers the rough
frayed fibres of his days and begins to mend
his world into stories that he discovers
these hostile mouths within his, and he reaches
down to drink through the roots of their rage. He begins
to see his enemies as he sees himself: as thirsty, as hungry, as
imprisoned by seemingly invincible histories.

And he tastes in his throat the deep thirst
of their grief, discerns the notes of their affliction
within each insult and barb.

When he has worn for a story the cloak
of their bile and knows in his skin
the abrasion of their sorrow, there arises for them
in his blood a self-pity. In a breath he asks
and grants their forgiveness, and he
is its source, its wound, its teller.

The Forgiving Manager

In a story Jesus tells, there's a manager
whose master catches him bleeding
the till — then lets the embezzler
settle the accounts. The manager forgives
great debts that are not his:
makes a thousand bushels of grain
six hundred and a thousand measures
of wine four hundred; tells each creditor
to record this, quickly, on his bill.
And the master applauds the manager's gall,
his use of his position to ease
the weight of credit on his neighbours.

Forgiveness is a mischief that anyone
can play, releasing one's cohorts
from the bonds of books — as Jesus
forgives payments never owed to him,
usurping undercover the prerogatives
of God. Any son or daughter of man
can do this. Who are *you*, he is asked,
to forgive a man's sins? He evades
the question, proclaiming simply that sins
are forgiven. It's not about authority.
It's about who dares to take the pen.

Talents

It was a kind of simulation game: each one given
a considerable sum to see how he could turn a profit.
The first two took seriously the ethics
of capital. Deaf to the pleas of their former
friends, they proved the first, self-evident
law of economics: that he who has most
will be given more. We're not informed
what their investments were, or whom
they impoverished, simply that they were successful
in the multiplication of funds.

But the third. All of the coins the master
had given him tinkled like water through his
well-intentioned hands, his allotment shared
with his neighbours for bread and for wells,
for payment of the doctor to save a sick child.

When the day comes to present their accounts,
the first two are settled in the waiting room
before him. They are clothed by the better
sort of tailor, one with a ten-fold heft of coins
rattling noisily in his purse and his head;
the other with only a five-fold profit
and berating himself for not making more.
The third has spread his treasure as profusely
as seed, magnanimously scattering its value to the wind.
In his cool disregard of impending accounts,

he has watched his money evaporate as mist.
He pities the wealthy in their seats beside him, each
of them chained to the whims of his purse, his vision
funnelled to the width of a coin.

He has turned the tables on the traders in money,
escaped from the cage of their counting and banks.
Flaunting his poverty's insolent freedom,
he needs no reward for the kingdom is his.

The Planter

The planter is exuberant, prodigal, free,
spilling seed where seed could never grow.
He tosses it upon the hard bodies of rocks,
who hold no wombs to bear its harvest.

He casts it to thin, inhospitable soil
and invites the thistles that would clutch at its throats.
He graciously feeds the needs of wild birds
who transplant the seeds in their generous dirt –

for there is, as the birds know, no infertile land.
Gifts are hurled out where they are not deserved,
and shoots sprout boldly where they have no right.
The planter is unstinting as the pourer of rain,

who grants it to desert and garden alike.
This fool sows blithely where he will not reap,
refusing to tally his planting's costs,
and scattering with a vast incalculable joy.

Flower and Flight

He was held, he knew, to the heart
of God as dearly as the sparrows
that scattered in the skies.

And the spirit, its fluttering into
his breast, was as warming and welcome
as the dove he'd watched settling

soft to her nest. As he spoke
he was enchanted by a lily and
uttered his purest line of poetry:

how Solomon in all his glory
was not arrayed like one
of these. His eye was called

to the wondrous in the given world:
This, he urged, and again,
See this, the earth surrendering

the spirit he strove for and offering it
freely, in flower and flight.
He'd look up from a story

to discover the sky, lift his eyes
like the rise of his body
in dreams. He would step

from the earth with the ease
of a bird and ascend to the spiralling
kingdom of heaven,

the air holding him safe
and swift and playing as he soared
and spun in the palm of its hand.

Indolence

First, consider the lilies
that neither sew nor spin
but sway in the breeze
and flaunt their fine clothing.

And consider Martha, bustling
with food and drink and worry
while Mary, her slow and dreamy-eyed
sister, reclines in ease at Jesus' feet.

Martha snaps that Mary won't help,
and Jesus murmurs, as he accepts
a plate from Martha, that her sister
has chosen the better part.

Men who have lolled in bed
past noon, then wandered down
to the market square – they
are paid precisely as much

for their one cool hour of work
as those who have laboured since dawn
through the furnace of the day.
C'est la vie, shrugs Jesus.

The prodigal's brother has toiled
every day for years on the farm.
His reward? To be standing alone
in a field at dusk and hear

the party for his dissolute brother
who shirked all work and opted
for pleasure, for wine in abundance
and prostitutes' skills.

Work results foremost in the sense
of deserving, a capital as handy
as the bulk of a camel, the curse
of the upright in every generation.

Work hard, counsels Jesus, and watch
your treasure rust on Earth.
Relax, have a drink.
Welcome to *la dolce vita*.

Children and the Kingdom

They've not fixed themselves in a single skin
or surrendered their wonder
to the world of needs – still intent
on entering the somewhere of stories,
where they are blessedly relieved
of themselves and stitched to the fabric
of another's skin. Craving their daily
turn in the ecstatic, they sojourn
in thoughts beyond their own and absorb
the tints of neighbouring minds. Supple
with becoming, they step
into stories' myriad rooms,
encountering the wondrous with
awakening eyes as they surge
toward bright, successive
births. They lose their lives
and receive them again, dissolving
to stories that exceed
and include them, that leave them
anonymous and newly named. Theirs
is the kingdom, worlds without end.

Reversals

For Jesus the world is made of water
and what now holds one form will soon hold another.
The male will be female, the straight will be bent,
the irreligious holy, and the righteous cast down.

The rich will lead another of their lives as the poor,
shifting positions like places at a table;
people slipping as in story to Samaritan skin
and feasting with the disparate citizens of heaven.

Jesus coolly enacts the drama of his words,
taking the roles of eunuchs and girls:
serving food and washing his followers' feet,
letting women of means foot all of his bills.

He becomes in his mind a clucking hen
who collects a brood beneath her wings.
Not contained as human, Jew, or male,
he adds and subtracts the cubits of stature.

He'd say: There is not one among you
but will find themselves altered, their flesh redefined,
the body of their poverty refashioned in gold.

For your souls are blessed with so many colours,
there is nothing in all the wardrobe of angels
which cannot be given to you as your skin.

Good News

We're redeemed by the speech
that emerges from our mouths,
language that remakes
the world toward beauty.

What restarts our creation
is always the word, its gifts
hidden like birdsong
in the alphabet's lattice.

Our most ragged moments
are called to the party,
our buried treasure
drawn up from the dirt.

There is not in our past
one single stray sheep or misplaced
coin but is ready to take
its place in a shining.

Each one of our seeds
is planted and spoken,
expanding into orchards
and stanzas of light.

Again

What delights you have given me,
        give me again. Give me again
those trials in the desert, that impulse
        to hurl myself down toward death.
Give me labour on pig farms, gnawing
        of hunger, assault on the road
and blood in my mouth. Repeat each conscription,
        double its distance, reiterate
the savage patterns of scorn. Strike me
        again, on my second cheek. Spare me
nothing of trouble or test. Let me know
        and be stained by every forgivable
sin in your book, by each blindness
        that succumbs to the tumbling of light.
Whatever you've done to me,
        do it again. Don't deny me one
of your blows, your blessings. Give me
        the world in its riches again.

Perfume

With all of a prostitute's
    attention to the senses,
she pours out the jar
    of her body for Jesus,
cascading her sorrow over
    his feet and praising
with the generous rain
    of her tears. She bathes
his feet in rich oil
    of myrrh, that ancient calm
and faint provocation.
    Sheets of her hair
descend on his ankles,
    and she burnishes
the gentle slopes
    of his feet. She's become
the most treasured
    of heaven's rags.
She anoints him bountifully
    with the pleasures of flesh,
turning her earnings
    to the wine of perfume,
a gift that caresses
    the spirit with scent.
Her hands as they soothe
    his weary feet plant him

again in the soil
    of his senses. For
this she will always
    hold her place in his story.

Better Not to Marry

Jesus, speaking to his intimate
circle of friends, assures them
it's better not to marry
but to wander unfamilied
in the company of men. He calls
his merry band to not-marry
with him, and conceives
of a Creator who, from the womb,
fashions this unmarrying brand of men
and calls them as prophets
in the birth of a kingdom.

Jesus extols the flexible eunuch
who sets aside his masculine habits
and surrenders himself to the wills
of men. He wishes all his followers
to be men and eunuchs, blessed
with that angelic ambiguity
of gender as they are entered
and enter the gates of heaven.

Jesus looks forward to that far
resurrection when marriage itself
will be finally moulted
and all will float freely
as bachelors and boys.
They'll drift promiscuous

through heavenly forms,
their bodies as permeable
and as shimmering as words.

A Woman Caught in Adultery

It was his hands
that seduced me from fidelity and made me
an idol within my own skin. I knew then
what lilies know
when they open wide their throats in praise;
I knew exultation as birds that chorus
in the tree of my flesh.
If this – *this* – was sin, it was thick
with God's choosing. I knew then how delight
could gambol through
the mountains of the body, how a woman,
quickened, is made in God's image.
My spirit ascended
like steam from a meal. And I looked down,
as from a great height, on the glittering fragments
of Mosaic law,
its pieces beautiful and edged with sorrow,
a beloved homeland I must leave behind.
I'd woken
to a tambourined dancing in my blood,
to anklets like stars that rang out with joy.
And I in this
act I'd been warned of all my life,
I was pure and profuse and guiltless as gold.

This Jesus eyes me, not like merely another
suitor, but like a woman who shares
my knowledge of men, who's set foot

on several of the narrow roads to God.
His face before me holds not condemnation
but a bodily knowledge. I know

that he would do as I've done. Languorous
as a poet recalling his beloved,
he writes on earth as if tracing

love's letters on skin. Called back
to the place where I stand, he faces me,
me with sweet saliva still slick

on my skin, my lover's adoration
polishing my limbs. He murmurs to be
careful not to sin, and I may never sin

again. It is shared in our eyes. We have
both tasted forbidden honey and know
that the hive of God is well-pleased.

Jesus, Versatile

Jesus, slippery from the beginning,
    becomes the wholly versatile man:
entering, entered, everywhere
    at once. His wish has always
been for inclusion, with God
    in him and he in God –
twisting, elaborate, androgynous,
    serpentine – his friends in him
and him in them, all perfectly
    permeable, perfectly one.

God like a genie slips
    into Jesus, lighting his skin
with the lamps of the temple
    and polishing all the fine
chambers inside him. God is
    the swimming who enters
his belly and expands in an ocean
    where he circles and breeds.

And Jesus, in awe at this
    sacred consent, eases himself
into God's rich body, sliding
    in the dark of his father's
womb, breathing a holiness
    from before his birth
and moving in the tenderest
    realms of the world.

Jesus enters like strange music
   the flesh of his friends,
disarming each in turn as he crosses
   the questioning borders of their lips
and insinuates himself
   in the memories of their flesh.
He's inside them like bones
   being slowly reclothed.

These men are granted entrance
   to his inner castle,
their washed feet walking
   the halls of his heart,
parting as he yields
   the most precious of tapestries,
as he calls each one of them
   gently by name.

Jesus is arrayed in the splendour
   of a bridegroom and bride,
versed in all pleasures earthly
   and divine. His lips are inviting,
lavish with desire and hued
   with every nuance of love.

Jesus, Praying

It comes to him mainly in the gathering of darkness
when he feels the sky stretch the wineskin of his chest

and he breathes in the textures of night-breeze and leaf,
these monochrome colours all silver and black.

This is where the doors of his skin are opened.
He yields himself to the brushing of wind

as it passes and flutes through the air of his bones.
He's one small, expanding lung of the night;

his throat is opened like a gorge to the starlight,
and his thirst is nourished by these draughts of dark.

He's a creature manoeuvring through black oceans of air,
learning these firmaments that lap him like tongues.

He's a man and impossibly more than a man,
as abundantly graced as a broad pride of angels,

as cool and poised and as pleasured with air.
He's ascended from his day to this spiralling mountain,

to this night that deepens the colour of his blood
and leaves him nearly drunk with black-scented breath.

Tonight he is older than the first of his fathers,
a witness to the earliest days of creation.

He is.

The Transfiguration

When Jesus ascends to the height of the mountain,
there are with him in a brilliance two men
who like him have been scalded and exalted
by light. There, with alert and finely
tuned ears, his face with the human
features of radiance, and his lips
like the blazing fierce mouth
of the sun, is the Prophet.
Beside him in blue
and cool clear light
is the seated flower poise of Buddha,
his smile perched like a bird
on his body's tree.

Muhammad speaks in ambered tones,
his every cadence a considered gift,
and behind the footfall of each of his lines,
animals cross the desert of his heart. His words
are composed in crafted precision,
in the patterns of a stellar geometric
complexity. He speaks with a sure
and humoured gleam, as if sacred
script from a dream were massaging
and delighting the backs of his eyes.

And the Buddha, composed,
blossoms his words from a bowlful

of silence, unfolding phrases with the flesh
of petals. His voice resounds from a luminous
history that treasures each one of his
animal lives, the years as monkey, turtle, deer.
The words of Buddha soak
as rain soaks deep to soil,
dispersing to leave
that stillness and scent.

And Jesus with the playful
charm of his lips is casting the nets
of another new story, directing
their eyes to the flash of bright details,
to stray sheep and quick snakes and the lift
in the breeze. He pours
out his voice like a jar
of perfume, indulging his listeners'
ears and feet, as he scatters
his speech with small lilies of beauty.

Peter, James, and John are listening, their minds
    overflowing
with more of the sacred than their cups
can hold. No greater magnitude than any one
of these men could be imagined, and yet these three
have trebled it among them. The followers of Jesus
scramble to find shelter for these figures
in their minds – to hold in one moment
what cannot be held. This,
says a voice in the three quaking men,
this is where my favour

rests. Listen to what these mouths
reveal. And Peter and James and John
exclaim, as they will for the rest
of their lives, How good it is that we are here.

Lazarus

Krishna with all his bodily beauty
    is reclining deep inside the tomb,
slumbering on the rocky serpent of the Earth;
    and Jesus proceeds on the long road toward him.
Krishna is wrapped in strips of gravecloth,
    his skin moist with the fragrant oils of death.
Each summons the other from across the rock,
    which is loosed by the falling tears of Jesus,
by the yearnings of Krishna as he lies like stone.
    The lithe mind of Krishna is calling for Jesus
as Jesus cries out for the stone to be moved.
    Krishna rises like mist to his dancer's posture
and draws Jesus on with his mind's silent music.
    Krishna is Jesus' long-absent companion
who steps now with speechless beauty from the grave
    as Jesus is greeted by this searching blue face,
its shine of profuse and alluring life.
    They meet as bridegrooms long promised to each other,
as twins who slept coiled in the ages before birth.
    Jesus touches his lips to the lips of his friend,
as each scented petal they have seen or imagined
    descends and suffuses this scene of meeting.
And all the borders of both their worlds
    lie in exquisite ribbons at their feet.

Jesus Enters Jerusalem

There were few Jewish precedents for such love between men,
and his companions would often call him their David,
praise him as their shepherd, their harpist, their psalmist,
their king. Jesus was as bright as the face of young David,
with his proclivity to mischief, and that bloom on his cheeks.
When for the holiday their troupe enters Jerusalem,
one shouts out to Jesus on his donkey: Hail David!
Others raise their voices: All joy to King David,
Hosanna and blessings on David our king!
The band all joins in the impromptu theatrics,
fanning him with branches, casting cloaks before him –
picturing their powerless playboy as a king.

Roman soldiers are not well acquainted with David
but have ears sharply tuned for a word like *king*.
They've been ordered to be vigilant
for rumours of messiahs or royal claims.
The soldiers report this exuberant retinue.
Their superiors will charge Jesus with being a pretender,
taking improvised levity for an ill-guided coup.
Jesus will be condemned by his friends' affection;
his resemblance to David will prove his end.

Bread of His Body

His body, he knew, was food,
was manna, a gift and a nourishment
to those it fell to.
He'd dispense his body
as the clouds yield rain,
offering it to all
without distinction.

Take me, he says, and place me
in your mouths. Recline
as I'm welcomed into your body
and pour to the lacing
streams of your blood.

He is spread and pulled
by scores of fingers, raised in turn
to each man's lips,
mouthfuls of Jesus
corrupting the virility
of all his companions
as he's licked by the hunger
of a dozen tongues.

The Beloved Disciple

The beloved disciple has no name, stitching
    each postulant into the gospel as we nestle
        toward Jesus' shoulder and breath, resting
on the chest of our dearest friend. The beloved
    is the needle every reader slides through.
        Inside him we recline in the bodily
warmth of Jesus and gleam like an apple
    in the garden of his eye – glowing
        in the smile of our master's delight.

Judas

The love shared by his friends was not without jealousy.
They constantly vied for Jesus' affection –
bickering over who would sit by his side
or who that day was dearer to his heart.

It was Judas who most needed Jesus to himself.
He could not tolerate the sharing of his saviour,
his passing like bread to all at the table.
When he sees his dear beloved lord

reclining with another man's head on his chest,
the devil of betrayal enters his mind.
His skin broods with the memory of Jesus' own,
cannot bear this dallying with another man.

When Judas is offered thirty pieces of silver
as payment for his bitter betrayal of Jesus,
he imagines the perfumes he could buy for his master,
hoards the thought of him pouring these over his feet.

He plans his manoeuvres, revises his lines
so that Jesus will know how much he adores him.
When by night he approaches his friend in the garden,
his heart is in splinters with what he commits.

It is love that compels me to do this, he pleads;
declares this as clearly as he can, with a kiss.
Judas, a spurned and impetuous lover,
at once regrets what his passion has bred.

There's his frantic, operatic return of the silver,
his flinging it to the ringing flagstones of the temple:
coins he might have spent to save the poor.
But he cannot save the poor soul of himself.

He hangs himself like his victim from a tree,
joining with his loved one in the ritual of suicide –
climbing in his mind to the cross beside Jesus
that he might this day be with him in paradise.

Pilate's Wife Dreams of Jesus

He came as a stranger to the chamber of my dreams,
    and unlaced me with a husband's intimate skill.
His lips dripped with fresh aromatic honey
    that fell to the bloodied beauty of his skin
and left me thick with half-clotted love.
    He entered my bed like a lover, like a wound.
In silence he kissed me, his mouth underwater,
    and all the rules of breathing had changed.
He fingered my hair as sweetly as if I were dead,
    his scent as luxurious as the scent of a tomb,
frankincense wafting on the warmth of his skin.
    He feasted on blossoms I could taste in my mouth.
He passed over and through me like handfuls of air –
    and I kissed the delicious sweet face of my death.
He touched me with fingers that had grazed the sun
    and still echo inside me in their spreading of light.
I want only to join in his chorus of suffering,
    saying his strange name over in wonder.
He has turned me, a wife, to his virgin bride
    and stolen all memory of fidelity and shame.
I tell Pilate I've been troubled by this man in my dreams.
    I tell him that killing this man will kill nothing.
I know that all the basins of my household
    will not be enough to dissolve his sweet blood.

Pilate

Jesus stands accused
    of plucking at the prerogatives of the emperor
    by claiming the kingship of some Jewish ancestor.
Pilate and Jesus
    are surrounded by the ranks of soldiers and minions,
    and the rich asks the destitute if he's a king.
Jesus admits
    he's been a king when a story was told
    – adds that the kingdom was not of this world.
He tells Pilate
    that a man is given more than one birth,
    that each story yields its particular truth.
What is truth?
    asks Pilate, and Jesus again considers the sparrows,
    lets the weight of Pilate's question hang in the air.
What is truth?
    and Jesus plays stories before his eyes,
    meets Pilate with an arid Galilean silence.
Pilate is governor
    and acts, as he must, by a governor's agenda:
    he will make an example of this alleged pretender.
As he weighs
    the words and silence of this minor prophet,
    he composes the words to be hammered on his cross.
Pilate is inspired
    and venturing his version of truth, names Jesus
    the king of the kingless, the king of the Jews.

A Soldier Questions Jesus

Who holds the whip
that's lashing your back?

Whose foot was that
crumpling the backs of your knees?

Do you like it, little martyr,
when I spit in your face?

When I cuff you on one cheek
and then on the other?

Tell me, faggot,
who I am,

who is kicking you now
till you cough up your blood?

The Beloved and Mary at the Cross

The beloved stands with Mary at the foot
of the cross, supporting the grief
of his dear friend's mother. As blood

seeps out from Jesus' wounds,
the bonds of blood well up
within him, and he strains to peer

over his physical torment. Mother,
he says, there is your son.
And you, my beloved, there

is your mother. It's the nearest
with both his hands drilled
to the cross that he can

clasp a hand in his.
In words they are wed,
and his friend is made Mary's

beautiful son, as she's born
to a family she has not conceived,
her kinship extended by this bond

between men. The beloved is remade
as a wedding's wine and embraced
in the uttered nuptials of Jesus.

Jesus, Forsaken

The one purse of his mind has been pilfered of coins,
and black dogs tear at the scraps of his soul.

He is pinned on the horizon, an exemplum of failure,
and a poisonous loathing courses through his veins.

That his whole life could sour as a jar full of milk,
turn the noses and stomachs of those who'd revered him.

Cold darkness seeps in through the plates of his skull,
and he's drowning in the turbid waters of disgust.

He hangs as a remnant of belief's deceptions,
suffering the futile dark stink of death.

This is the closing tableau of his life.
Whatever he has done and said has been wrong.

Corpse

A man named Joseph cradles Jesus
    in his arms. Beside him huddles
Nicodemus, who once asked Jesus
    how a man can re-enter
his mother's womb. They tend
    to the brutalized body of Jesus,
tender as the foreigner
    who met a ravaged man
on the road. They soothe his body
    with oil and herbs, the air
fragrant with myrrh as it was
    at his birth; and their lotions
smooth the years from his face.
    The two men commune with this
one silent body, its mouth now
    a sorrow they will never forget.
They wrap its weight in swaddling
    cloth and together place Jesus
into his tomb as they hum
    him lullabies, stroke his brow.

The Angel at the Tomb

is the same young man of the torchlit skin
who sprinted from the sudden grip of soldiers,
leaving his strand of white linen in their hands.

When Jesus was kissed and seized in the garden,
reclining beside him, a smooth virgin pearl,
was this nameless man in his moonlit film.

He had sat all but naked by Jesus' side,
his posture toward him angelically intimate,
his secret folded in him like the smile of wings.

And now on this glorious morning at the tomb
he proclaims his beloved, resplendent with life:

and his joy dances nearly naked before them
as he carols the news his senses have witnessed.

His lips, so recently parted in pleasure,
reveal an exquisite knowledge of his friend;

he smiles a disarming, death-defying smile
and unspools his golden spoken ribbon of hope:

Jesus will find you, the youth-angel says,
and you too will blaze in the tongues of his light.

After

His thoughts as elaborate as the flight paths of sparrows,
as riddled with those urgent exclamations of joy –

he wakes to the implausible germination of seeds
that were scorched and pecked and trampled to death.

Colours are dense with the pleasures of themselves,
and birdsong is pitched to the intervals inside him.

His body is as lovely as long-awaited rain,
his soul thickly planted with abundant gold crops –

a fortune so expansive it blooms like yeast
and cannot be hidden in a hundred loaves.

His heart is clothed in the vestments of lilies,
and the riches of Solomon stream from his tongue.

Peter, Swimming

When Jesus had approached
his boat in the night, Peter was drenched
to redemption at the sight, wanting only
to join his companion on the water,
the two of them walking
and dancing on the waves, the world
an abyss defied
at their feet. They'd balanced
on the waves, the night breeze
sheeting the robes to their skin –
and they'd shattered
all their world's natural laws.
But Peter could not sustain this
for long. He'd fallen,
sinking to his ankles and knees,
unable to uphold the required belief.

Now, as he's hauling up
nets from the sea, he's told that the man
on the beach is Jesus, and Peter
is no longer afraid of falling. He plunges
in his nakedness into the lake
and drenches himself again to reach
Jesus. He swims among fish
and strokes as men
do not do in his world, opening
his eyes in this second element

and surging inside this liquid life.
He's cleansed of all denials
that he'd accompanied Jesus.
He is wet and strong and male
and forgiven. Peter swims naked
toward Jesus on the shore
and this time there's no shame
that can cause him to fall.

Thomas

A greater love than this has no man:
to open his body for the faith of his friend.

Jesus is exuding a milky rich light,
the wicks of a hundred sacred virgins

trimmed and lit in the lamp of his skin.
He draws back his shoulder to expose his wound.

He won't resist the wondering fingers of his friends
or preserve a virginity by holding them back.

Jesus' love for Thomas is profuse, without limit,
as abundant as sunlight on a single lily.

Thomas is stricken and needs to press forward,
has never had such privilege poured into his skin.

He inhales the metallic sweet scent of redemption
and narrows his eyes to that narrow red door,

his finger hovering humbly at salvation's gate.
Jesus is as radiant as the face that meets the bridegroom

– is given by no one but himself and light.
He needs to instruct his novice lover:

Place your finger here, he says, gently, like that.
Let it entering coo as softly as a dove

and flicker with the tiny quick tongue of a snake.
Thomas probes slightly further than the spear had pierced

and as always for Jesus, for a moment, it hurts.
Thomas in his senses has stroked the eternal;

his finger has slipped to the kingdom of heaven,
and he can never return to a normal man's life.

As I Have Loved You

His eyes supplanted all we'd known
                              of family,
tugged us to childhood and again
                              to first love.
He rewrote our most hidden desires
                              as sacred
and led us to heaven through the gate
                              of his skin.
He loved us each with a singular
                              devotion,
as if we were the treasure
                              he had always sought.
He'd draw clean bliss to the surface
                              of our skin
as if hauling up nets that glistened
                              with fish.
He'd pillow beneath us the dreams
                              of his stories,
casting our attention to wave-flash
                              and phrase –
coaxing us to inhabit his kingdom
                              of change.

He'd asked us to love others as he
                              had loved us,
and we share among strangers the faith
                              they're adored,

that the world's eyes delight
                    in seeing them live.
We ignite others' faces with the fire
                    of stories —
and here he is again, brilliant
                    in our midst.
His presence has called us, as friends
                    are called,
to bring beauty to blaze in the eyes
                    of companions,
to unclothe their lives with language
                    and love.

Appearances

Mary Magdalene held the features of Jesus
clutched like an icon in the fist
of her heart. And Jesus appears
to her as the gardener, the bones
of his face all newly replanted.
To the searching disciples, he's a
shimmering young man; to others
an arrogant traveller who sits down
for a meal. Disguised as an aging man
mending his nets, he tells weary fishermen
where to cast down, his identity proven
by the weight of their catch.

Delighting in the mischief of masquerade,
he toys with his disciples' religious
plasticity. When he plays a prostitute
or a woman by the well, his male friends
stare, shake their heads, turn away,
won't admit this to the text
as a sighting of their lord.
And the women are reviled when they claim
they have seen him. He has instigated
the game of *Where's Jesus?*
that people will play for thousands
of years, finding him with surprise
in pariahs and foreigners, in children
and foxes and birds of the air.

Jesus Not Contained in His Book

The gospels close by affirming their faith
in fiction. If all the imagined acts of Jesus
were to be made elaborate and laid out on paper,

these tales would far outstrip his brief life,
and the world itself could not contain
the countless books that should be written.

His life, like the trick with the bread and
the fish, yields abundantly more in leftover baskets
than it offered at first in its unbroken food.

His stories persist in reshaping themselves,
adapting their contours to the questions they're posed
as his memory spreads among us like weeds.

They invite the new twist of another
translation, the angling of his phrases to a new
tone of light. His words breed profusely

in foreign soil, creating miscegenate, bastardized
gospels as he consorts with the sages
of foreign faiths and commits his egregious

religious adulteries. He dances in scandalous
rhythms of praise, and the library of his lives
cannot be completed, the ever-sinuous

body of Jesus coiling and recoiling
itself into lines, contorting into gospels
apocryphal and rare – shaping each novel

chaos into the order of chapter and verse.
With Jesus we create from our own desecration,
hauling up what was hidden in the filth of our lives.

We step beyond Jesus' steps on the water,
striding the unending lake of revelation,
the light of him shaved into sheets of words.

Biblical References

Mt: Matthew
Mk: Mark
Lk: Luke
Jn: John
Jesus, Son of David: Mt. 1.1, I Samuel 18-20, II Samuel 1, 6, 11
The Conversion of Jesus: Lk. 3.21-23, 15.11-32
Jesus and the Foreign: Lk. 10.25-37
Spit and Blindness: Mk. 8.22-26
Jairus' Daughter: Mk. 5.21-24, 35-43
Healed of Haemorrhages: Mk. 5.24-34
Jesus Seeking Solitude: Mk. 1.35, 1.45, 3.10, 3.20, 6.31
Jesus, Suicidal: Mt. 4.5-7, Lk. 8. 26-33, 15.3-6
Jesus Considers Amputation: Mt. 5.29-30, 18.8-9
Corruption: Lk. 13.18-21, Mk. 8.15, Genesis 18.22-33
Weeds: Mt. 13.24-30
Open Party: Lk. 7.33-34, 14.12-24
Tax Collectors: Lk. 5.27-32
Snake of God: Jn. 3.14-15, Exodus 20.4, Numbers 21.4-9
The Mother of Jesus: Mk. 3.31-35, Lk. 14.26
Enemies: Mt. 5.43-48, 11.16-17, 23.23-24
The Forgiving Manager: Lk. 16.1-8
Talents: Mt. 25.14-30, Jn. 2.13-16
The Planter: Mk. 4.3-9, Mt. 5.44-45
Flower and Flight: Mt. 3.16, 6.26-29
Indolence: Lk. 12.22-31, 10.38-42, Mt. 20.1-16, Lk.15.11-32
Children and the Kingdom: Mk. 10.13-16, Jn. 3.1-7, Lk. 9.24
Reversals: Lk. 6.20-26, 8.1-3, 13.30, 13.34-35, 22.26-27, Jn. 13.3-10
Good News: Mk. 7.14-15, Lk. 17.21, Jn. 1.1-3, Mt. 13.44
Again: Mt. 5.38-42

Perfume: Lk. 7.37-38, Mk. 14.3-9
Better Not to Marry: Mt. 19.10-12, 22.29-30
A Woman Caught in Adultery: Jn. 8.2-11
Jesus, Versatile: Jn. 14.10-11, 14.20, 17.20-26
Jesus, Praying: Lk. 5.16, 6.12, Jn. 8.58
The Transfiguration: Mt. 17.1-8
Lazarus: Jn. 11.1-44
Jesus Enters Jerusalem: Mt. 21.1-9, Mk. 11.9-10, Lk. 19.38
Bread of His Body: Mt. 26.26
The Beloved Disciple: Jn. 13.23
Judas: Jn. 13.21-27, 12.4-6, Mt. 26.14-16, 26.47-50, 27.3-5
Pilate's Wife Dreams of Jesus: Mt. 27.19
Pilate: Jn. 18.33-19.22
A Soldier Questions Jesus: Lk. 22.63-65
The Beloved and Mary at the Cross: Jn. 19.26-27
Jesus, Forsaken: Mk. 15.29-34
Corpse: Jn. 19.38-42, 3.1-4, Lk. 2.7, 10.29-37, Mt. 2.11
The Angel at the Tomb: Mk. 14.51-52, 16.5-8
Peter, Swimming: Jn. 21.4-8, Mt. 14.22-33, 26.69-75
Thomas: Jn. 20.24-29
As I Have Loved You: Jn. 13.34, 15.11-17
Appearances: Jn. 20.10-18, 21.4-13, Lk. 24.13-31, Mk. 16.12, Mt. 25.31-46
Jesus Not Contained in His Book: Jn. 21.25, Mk. 6.38-44

Acknowledgements

The translations of the gospels that I have used most are:
The New English Bible
The New Revised Standard Version
The King James Version

The books that have been most helpful in providing information and ideas are:
The Silence of Jesus by James Breech (Toronto: Doubleday, undated)
Jesus: A Revolutionary Biography by John Dominic Crossan (New York: HarperCollins, 1994)
The Gospel According to Jesus by Stephen Mitchell (New York: HarperCollins, 1991)
Profiles of Jesus edited by Roy W. Hoover (Santa Rosa: Polebridge, 2002)
The Last Temptation of Christ by Nikos Kazantzakis (New York: Simon and Schuster, 1960)
Meeting Jesus Again for the First Time by Marcus Borg (New York: HarperCollins, 1994)
Reading the Bible Again for the First Time by Marcus Borg (New York: HarperCollins, 2001)
From Jesus to Christ by Paula Fredriksen (New Haven: Yale, 1988)
The Five Gospels by Robert W. Funk, Roy W. Hoover, and the Jesus Seminar (New York: HarperCollins, 1997).

"Better Not to Marry" first appeared in *The Malahat Review* and in *Seminal* (Arsenal Pulp Press, 2007). "Open Party" first appeared in *Descant*. This book was produced with the support of the Ontario Arts Council. Thanks to Antonio D'Alfonso, Janet McClelland, and Bryan Young.